QUÉBEC

JOURNEY ACROSS CANADA

Harry Beckett

The Rourke Book Co., Inc.
Vero Beach, Florida 32964

Harry Beckett M.A. (Cambridge), M.Ed. (Toronto), Dip.Ed. (Hull, England) has taught at the elementary and high school levels in England, Canada, France, and Germany. He has also travelled widely for a tour operator and a major book company.

Edited by Laura Edlund
Laura Edlund received her B.A. in English literature from the University of Toronto and studied Writing for Multimedia and Book Editing and Design at Centennial College. She has been an editor since 1986 and a traveller always.

ACKNOWLEDGMENTS
For photographs: Geovisuals (Kitchener, Ontario), The Canadian Tourism Commission and its photographers.
For reference: *The Canadian Encyclopedia, Encarta 1997, The Canadian Global Almanac, Symbols of Canada. Canadian Heritage*, Reproduced with the permission of the Minister of Public Works and Government Services Canada, 1997.
For maps: Promo-Grafx of Collingwood, Ont., Canada.

Library of Congress Cataloging-in-Publication Data

Beckett, Harry. 1936 -
   Québec / by Harry Beckett.
     p. cm. — (Journey across Canada)
   Includes index.
   Summary: An introduction to the geography, history, economy, major cities, and interesting sites of Canada's largest province that is seven times larger than Great Britain.
   ISBN 1-55916-201-5 (alk. paper)
   1. Québec (Province)—Juvenile literature. [1. Québec (Province)]
I. Title II. Series: Beckett, Harry, 1936 - Journey across Canada.
F1052.4.B43 1997
971.4—dc21
                                     97-1422
                                     CIP
                                     AC

Printed in the USA

TABLE OF CONTENTS

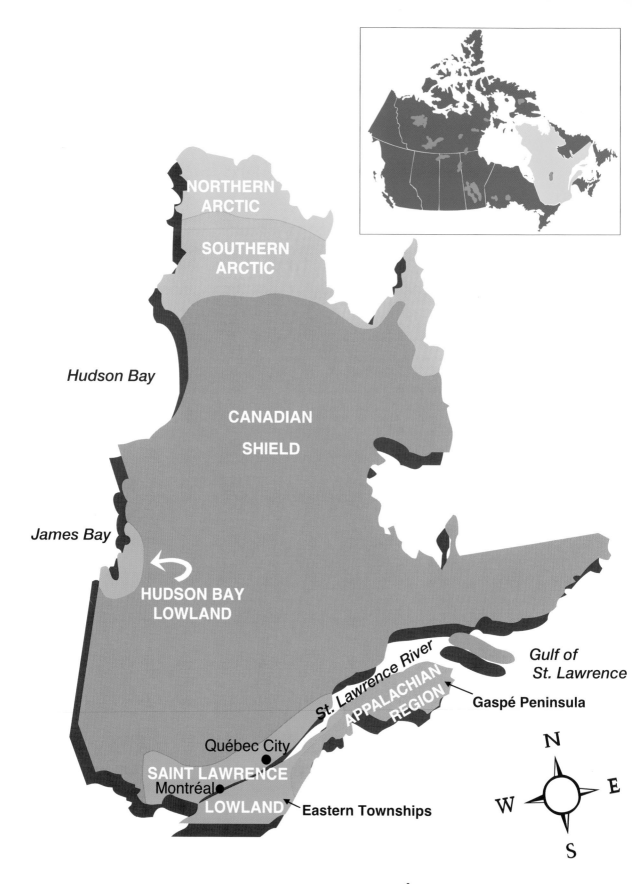

NORTHERN
ARCTIC

SOUTHERN
ARCTIC

Hudson Bay

CANADIAN

SHIELD

James Bay

HUDSON BAY
LOWLAND

*Gulf of
St. Lawrence*

St. Lawrence River

APPALACHIAN
REGION

Gaspé Peninsula

Québec City

SAINT LAWRENCE

Montréal

LOWLAND

Eastern Townships

N

W E

S

PROVINCE OF QUÉBEC

Chapter One

SIZE AND LOCATION

Québec is Canada's largest province—seven times the size of Britain and almost as large as Alaska.

Most of the people live along the St. Lawrence River, which divides the province into two unequal parts. The northern region is much larger than the southern region, which includes the Gaspé Peninsula and the Eastern Townships. After it passes Québec City, the river quickly becomes much wider as it approaches the Gulf of St. Lawrence and the Atlantic Ocean.

Hudson Bay and the border with Ontario are to the west of the province. New Brunswick and a part of Newfoundland called Labrador lie to the east. To the south are the American states of Maine, New Hampshire, Vermont, and New York.

Find out more...

• Québec is 1971 kilometres (1225 miles) from north to south and 1600 kilometres (994 miles) from east to west.

• Around seven million people live in the province.

5

Chapter Two

GEOGRAPHY: LAND AND WATER

A huge, rocky area of lakes, rivers, and forests, called the **Canadian** (kuh NAY dee un) **Shield** (SHEELD), covers four fifths of Québec.

The northern part of the Shield is **tundra** (TUN druh), home to polar bears, foxes, arctic hares, and thousands of caribou. Farther south is rich in wildlife such as moose, deer, and wolves. The Laurentian Mountains form the southern edge of this region.

The Canadian Shield north of the St. Lawrence

A family enjoys the Bon Secours Market in Old Montréal

Nine out of ten Québecers live in the **fertile** (FUR tile) St. Lawrence Valley, mostly in towns and villages. Montréal and Québec City are both on the St. Lawrence River.

To the south of the St. Lawrence is an area of old mountains. The forests of these regions are **deciduous** (duh SIJ oo us). The Eastern Townships and the Gaspé lie in this area.

Chapter Three

WHAT IS THE WEATHER LIKE?

The very cold and snowy winters of Québec made life difficult for early settlers. Today, people have learned to enjoy the pleasures winter can bring, and skiing, snowmobiling, and hockey are very important parts of Québec life.

The province is very large, so each region has its own climate. The far north has about nine months of frosty days, and the summers are short and remain cool. In Montréal, there is snow on the ground for about four months, but the winters move quickly into pleasant, enjoyable summers.

Fall in the southern forests, when the leaves turn yellow and brilliant red, is a glorious season.

Find out more...

- Montréal has average temperatures of -6°C (21° F) in January and 26°C (79° F) in July.
- In Québec's far north temperatures are -23°C (-9.4° F) and 11°C (52° F).

At the Québec Winter Carnival, the mascot, le Bonhomme, and his friends enjoy the snow.

8

Chapter Four

MAKING A LIVING: HARVESTING THE LAND

Québec is large but does not have much farmland. Its farms are mostly in the St. Lawrence Valley or the Eastern Townships, where the land is fertile and the growing season is quite long.

Many Québec farms look like ribbons stretching from the rivers. Early settlers saw the land on the river edge as very important. It was fertile, and the river was a canoe route in summer and sled route in winter.

Farms are small, but the government has helped them to work together. Grain, vegetable, and beef production has grown. Québec has more dairy farms than any other province. Poultry, eggs, apples, and soft fruits are also important.

Québec's huge forests provide wood products, and its maple syrup is world famous.

Farms close together along rivers or roads make mail delivery and schoolbusing easy.

Find out more...

- This farm system is called the seigneurial system, named for the landowners granted land by the king of France.
- Fields are 175.5 metres (576 feet) wide but over 1700 metres (more than a mile long).

Chapter Five
FROM THE EARLIEST PEOPLES

When Jacques Cartier landed in 1534, the Native peoples who met him were farmers. They were driven out by hunter-gatherers by the time Champlain arrived in 1608.

Few French colonists arrived at first, but slowly the land was settled and fur traders built the fur trade. However, contact with Europeans brought diseases and death to many Native peoples.

Coureurs de bois in their furs and buckskins

Early settlers may have crossed the ocean in a boat like this one.

The population began to grow, especially at the time of the American Revolution (1775-83), when people loyal to Britian moved north. General Wolfe's victory on the Plains of Abraham gave Britain control of the region.

Many Québecers who descend from the French settlers consider themselves a **distinct society** (dih STINGKT suh SY ih tee), and are proud of their **heritage** (HER ih tij).

13

Chapter Six

MAKING A LIVING: FROM INDUSTRY

Québec generates most of its electricity from its many rivers. It has no gas, coal, or oil of its own.

Industries often develop where power is close to natural resources. The province is rich in minerals, which it processes and sells.

Most other industry is in the Montréal area. The biggest industries are clothing and textiles, food and beverage, and pulp and paper industries.

The St. Lawrence River is Québec's spine. Ocean-going ships sail up it and through the St. Lawrence Seaway to the Great Lakes. Rivers link it to the north, and roads and railways run along its valley.

Find out more...

- One hydro-electricity project is the huge James Bay Project, which has caused problems for the Cree nation.
- Other industries are pulp, paper, aluminum, and iron ore.

Mill with piles of logs to be ground down into wood pulp for paper

14

Chapter Seven

IF YOU GO THERE...

Visit Old Québec City, with its **citadel** (SIT uh del) and fortified walls, and the Plains of Abraham. In summer, musicians perform in the streets and artists sell their paintings. During Winter Carnival there are ice sculptures, a huge ice palace, and teams racing in canoes across the partly frozen St. Lawrence.

Montréal, too, has its old town. Visitors can also enjoy an international comedy festival, rock and classical concerts, a Canadiens' ice hockey game, or an Expos' baseball game.

There is excellent skiing at Mont-Sainte-Anne and Mont-Tremblant. Everywhere there are lakes, beautiful countryside, and pleasant villages.

Ice sculpture, with ice palace, at the Québec Winter Carnival

17

Find out more...

- St. Joseph's Oratory is a landmark in Montréal.
- The village of Percé and its famous rock on the Gaspé Peninsula attract many tourists.

Chapter Eight

MAJOR CITIES

Québec City, the provincial capital, is a French-speaking city. Parts of it date from the seventeenth century, and the United Nations has named it a World Heritage Site. It has an inland seaport and an international airport.

Montréal is Canada's second-largest city and next to Paris, the world's biggest **francophone** (FRANG kuh fone) city and it hosted the 1976 Olympic Games and the 1967 World Exposition.

The Olympic Stadium in Montréal

Cannons overlook the river in front of the Hotel Chateau Frontenac in Québec City

Once the centre of the fur trade, Montréal is now known for its designer clothing. Ships from all over eastern North America pass through it as they sail along the St. Lawrence Seaway.

Both cities, with their universities, museums, theatres, restaurants, and **joie de vivre** (zhwah duh VEEV ruh), are good places in which to live.

Chapter Nine
SIGNS AND SYMBOLS

Québec's flag is made up of a white cross on a blue background. This is an old French military banner. The four fleur-de-lis in the corners represent France.

On the coat of arms, the three gold fleurs-de-lis on a blue background again recall early ties with royal France. The golden lion shows the province's ties with British royalty, and the maple leaves are from the Québec forest.

The French motto "Je me souviens," means "I remember."

The provincial flower, the white garden lily, does not grow naturally in Canada. It was chosen because it looks like the fleur-de-lis.

Québec's flag, coat of arms, and flower

JE ME SOUVIENS

GLOSSARY

Canadian Shield (kuh NAY dee un SHEELD) — a horseshoe-shaped area of rock covering about half of Canada

citadel (SIT uh del) — a fortress protecting a town

deciduous (duh SIJ oo us) — trees that lose their leaves every year

distinct society (dih STINGKT suh SY ih tee) — a group of people different from the rest, for example, because of its customs and history

fertile (FUR tile) — rich, good for growing things in

francophone (FRANG kuh fone) — French speaking

heritage (HER ih tij) — something passed down from earlier generations

joie de vivre (zhwah duh VEEV ruh) — French, meaning joy in living, enjoyment in life

tundra (TUN druh) — a treeless, arctic plain that remains frozen all year, except just at the surface

Boiling sap from the maple tree to make maple syrup

INDEX